Before the Next Song

and other Poems

First published in Zimbabwe by Mambo Press Publishers in 1999.

This edition was published in Great Britain in 2021 by:

Carnelian Heart Publishing Ltd

Suite A

82 James Carter Road

Mildenhall

Suffolk

IP28 7DE

UK

www.carnelianheartpublishing.co.uk

Paperback ISBN 978-1-8380480-8-2

Ebook ISBN 978-1-8380480-9-9

A CIP catalogue record for this book is available from the British Library.

Proofread by Samantha Rumbidzai Vazhure

Cover design: Rebecca Covers

Typeset by Carnelian Heart Publishing Ltd

Layout and formatting by DanTs Media

A note from the publisher

We consider this poetry collection to be a classic work of art that has attracted a lot of attention, including being made an A level set book for secondary schools in Zimbabwe. Having gone out of print, we were interested in republishing the work, because such a gem in African literature was worth reviving. This collection holds 31 poems split into 6 sections:

Savannah man

The house of brown glass

African tears are everywhere

Dreams about women

So, Let it be

Organising lines of poetry

While this edition does not include the commentary included in the first edition by Stanley Tichapondwa, minimal footnotes have been added, to facilitate easier interpretation of some of the more abstract poems.

Acknowledgements

The poems in this collection were originally published by Mambo Press Publishers in 1999. The original publication included a critical commentary on by Stanley Tichapondwa.

To the memory of my dear mother
Mrs. Josephine Chihota (*nee* Tapi).

Contents

Savannah Man

Savannah Man

I once sat next to a man
Who smelt like the morning-after's mouth
But the words which came out of his dry donga-bed lips
Sparkled like wavelets of the Mupfure
Playing early-morning games
With the summer sun.

Song of the Savannah Dove

We sat under leafy *mopane* trees and bickered
About names of colourful birds that twittered
In tall *musasas* nearby.
Scented was the Savannah that season
The musk
Of last year's husks
   Eaten like rusks
      In bristling ant-hills…
The perfume
Of long-necked, remontant flowers
Swooning in the breeze…
The strong anti-perspirant
Worn by impis of maturing elephant grass.…

The bored bellow of an old ancestral bull
Mellowing with age and sunshine
Unrolled over the grassland
Like a heavy quilt
Pressing everything to sleep.

Were we in dreamland?
Or succumbing to the suck of its quicksands
When this hoary, gory, grieving and heaving dove
Injured but hindered by love
Spoke of leaving
For the shimmering firmament above:

> *Paddock,*
> *Paddock your thoughts my sons*
> *Paddock your thoughts my sons*

Like those young acacia trees
Cream-soda green
That scream in their dreams
But only sigh
When they wake.

We were told not to trust our catapults
Or aim stones at the breasts of old grieving doves
We were warned not to be like Piasi
Who attacks others for no reason
And thus confused the seasons.

*Piasi is an abstract character in a childhood song sung by children in Mount Darwin, Zimbabwe, where the poet grew up. The song imitates the cooing of doves and was sung as follows:

"Kurururwi,

chandaroverwa

naPiasi

tsakata" (translation: "Kukurururwi/ I cannot understand/ why Piasi/ would want to attack me."

When the Rain Fell

When the rain fell last year
it beat upon burnt stubs of grass
raised black dust
swallowed it up
and washed it down brown swirling rivers.

When the rain fell this year
it beat upon burnt stubs of grass
raised black dust
chocked
coughed
and spluttered

Before retreating in a panic to the sky
where it hung back in fear
and vowed not to return
for the next three seasons.

The rain said 'No'
even after the clouds promised
to provide a protective mask.

*The final stanza was added to capture the recent experience of the
COVID19 pandemic

Land of the Sun

I

In that land
In that hot, hot land
The sun bites with razor-sharp teeth.
Its rays
Eat into the expecting mother's womb
To burn and blacken
The sweating foetus.

In that land
Old baobabs sigh
They sigh in aching susurrations.
Below them
Bleached skeletons of desiccated grass
Rattle and shimmer like a stretched carpet of death.

Rocks
Their burning backs humped above the ground
Wish to dive beneath the soil
They hiss and crackle cantankerously
At any chance drop of moisture
(a ball of hot saliva for instance)
That dares to tantalise them.

In that land
Dry stream beds
Smoulder shyly
Their exposed bottoms

Lying limply in the ground.

And snakes
Feeling their hot poison boil
Strike at each other
Like curling heated fingers
They die
Trying to swallow each other
Down the biltong walls
Of their parched throats.

In that land
There are no cattle.
The thin rheumy contraptions in hide
That stumble from hut to crumbling hut
Stealing grey ashy thatch
Represent what used to be cattle,
While dogs
Dull,
Infirm
And too weak to bark
Can only stare
At these phantasmagorical creatures
With dreamy and watery eyes.

II

In that land
In that hot, hot land
Was a small 'Upper Top' School
    A mirage

Of white square blocks
A crooked pattern
Of almost bare rockeries
(with a few cacti providing the greenery)
A multicoloured sign emblazoned
WELCOME TO MAKWATI HIGH.

In Makwati High's dusty yard
Teachers slaked
Like thirsty ostriches
Weeping sandy tears
Out of screwed, inflamed eyes.
And school children:
Their chapped lips snarling whitely
Their cracked feet harbouring bits and pieces
Their shorts and knickerbockers split on the behind
Like rude overripe peaches,
These
They stumbled from the hinterland of falling huts
To crawl back again
After each dry and emaciating day.

III

In that land
In that hot, hot land
In the dusty precincts of Makwati High
Molly watched her permed hair melt
Into a dark and fibrous margarine
Her red lips
Burst and peeled

Like fetid tomatoes
Ulcerating in the heat.

Molly's soul
Of long sleek cars,
Of psychedelic lights
Of sweets and ice-cream
Burnt and withered
And wilted under the sun.

But Suzie
The plain, hymn-singing Suzie,
She flourished like a showered shoot of lettuce
And watered with love
The burning world around her.

The Moholi Lemur

Child of the Savannah
born, breast-fed and raised by the grassland

You ran errands for your mother one morning
Dusting the barky branches of old baobabs
Nursing nascent flowers on frightened virgin bushes
Paying social visits to lonely loquat dowagers…

 In your brisk activity
You must have shed a large sweat drop,
Or else wiped a tear from a weeping willow leaf:
Something cold and wet fell
Right onto the nose
of the bully who led us.

We froze
Flared nostrils turned upwards
To smell the suspicious air.
Button-bright eyes
Lit with malice
Searched the foliage above us.

"There he is!"
"Take him!"
Nark and judge
Betrayer and sentencer….

Through the fork of my catapult

I saw you stare with huge moist eyes
That looked like saucers filled with water....

When you finally landed at our feet
A bleeding ball of fur
You still clutched a twiggy utensil
In one veined and hard-used paw.

As you breathed your last
Tears rained from the tree above us.

And,
As we slunk away
Puzzled
One Geographer among said
He could explain.

Hunter's Jogging Song

As I jog towards the bogs
I think about claws
Poking out of paws
Like arrows in a quiver
Printing pretty patterns on the mud of the river

Long feline claws
Drooping with languor
Tapering to points
Like little stalactites
Bright and shiny
Reflecting prisms
For the waning red rays of the sinking sun.

Like needles in a machine, meant to embroider
They printed other patterns on the earth behind the boulder
Fierce patterns
Warning of danger:
A skull and two bones crossing each other!

Long feline claws
Drooping with languor
Tapering to points, like brittle stalactites
Bright and shiny
reflecting prisms
for the waning red rays of the sinking sun.

Like shadufs tipped

To lift a trembling bucket
They tensed and tautened
And gripped like ratchets.
They whipped through the air
In arching flashes.
There was tearing
and shearing
and breaking of bone.
And redder than the sun
The claws now appeared!

> Long feline claws
> Drooping with languor
> Tapering to points like fickle stalactites
> Bright and shiny
> Reflecting prisms
> For the waning red rays of the sinking sun.

The House of Brown Glass

Before the Next Song

I
Delek, delek, delek
The juke-box coughs
Preparing to sing.
Has it drunk hot blood tonight?
(A scratch on the vinyl
Sends the stylus leapfrogging).

Smash!
    A quick hush
    Someone has broken
    His converted dollars.
        Like a snake
        That has paused to listen
        The noise pours out again.

Suddenly,
    Several perfumes rise
    They rush and waft around the room
    Like panicking widgeon
    Bristling amidst human grass.
        The beat
        Of a heavy pursuing order
        Marches past
        Like a clumsy posse
        Led by a blind, unwashed man.

At last

The box bursts into a tune
Deep baritone booms out
Slapping the ear wetly
Like sweat drops shaken
From an enemy's fist.

Feet and legs
Wet clay pillars
Sidle the dance floor.
Yellow eyes wink
Like a voyeur
Caught in the act.

II

Adam stumbles out of the *Wine and Wench*
The music still buzzing in his ears
Like a swarm of insistent *mopane* bees
Made of metal.

Wading in mercury
Adam forges ahead
Clutching the air for support
    Inshide
      Inshide de naitcub
      People are danshing
      People are performing
      Inshide the naitcub.

Lasered eyes in the dark
Pierce to the back of Adam's brain

Leaving potent venom.

A wall looms ahead
Heavily dressed in graffiti
Slogans and curses
Nicknames of the sacred
Jurassic Park monsters
Naked men and women
In flagrante delicto.

As Adam sweeps past
Life-size graffiti detaches itself
And clogs towards him on wooden soles.
    Ten bucks only
        Only ten bucks my honely.

The voice is crunchy and yet soft
Like gravel ladled with a polythene spoon.
Blood throbs in Adam's veins
Like Chitako-Cha-Ngonya's drums
Beating on new moon night.

Towards a dark copy-cat taxi
Crouching by the kerb
Adam steers his new-found Eve.

As they pile inside
To circumnavigate the night
Faint strains
Of the next song

This time
A dirge
Filter from the East
Of tomorrow.

Piddle Thoughts

Let's effect the demise of this wall
The piss seemed to hiss.

Let's jet upon that spot
Beneath the wall
And bequeath it with a burrow

Let's strike again and again
Until we form a furrow
That will sweep the wall away

Let's strike deeply and strongly
Until we meet the marrow
Of the earth....

So, it spouted out of three hissing hoses
Struck and scoured out the soft soil
Until it unearthed
A gleaming foundation stone.

The House of Brown Glass

To that cylindrical house we went
Voyagers vying for peace
In a world, empty as a sheath.

In that cone-roofed house we sat
Sojourners seeking solace and suckle
In a wilderness dry and teat-less
Like a knuckle

In that house of glass, we dwelt
To lubricate our minds
Delouse our spirits
And fumigate our souls

In that house of thick brown glass
we were refugees by choice
and charlatans, masking with noise
the little voice, whispering
that angst was here to stay.

Horns

I

Horns growing in my groins
Like extra gonads for my loins.

Horns swelling in my armpits and my neck
Like a synergy sudsing bubbles and wreck.

Horns whistling in my lungs
And choking my breath like bungs
Horns burgeoning in my brain
And burning my thoughts like acid rain.

Horns rustling
And tussling
In my spirit.

II

There is this barbed wire cough
That I scrape out of my lungs
With weakening bellows.

There is this dirigible diarrhoea
That blasts through the racecourse of my bowels
Cutting corners.

Then there is this cancer of the skin
That tattoos my body
In stupid places.
There is this
And that.

III

They say a warrior
Fights until his very guts
Spill out
And trail on the ground

They say a warrior
Parries blows with a strong arm
That induces alarm.

But which warrior can withstand
A whole battalion of attackers
Surrounding so thickly
They vie for spaces to land their blows?

And even if the warrior were to put up a fight
Which enemy from amongst the horde
Should he strike first?

IV

Is tuberculosis such a coward

It needed the company of diarrhoea
Before going out to hunt?
Is diarrhoea such a dunce
It needed to be led by cancer
Before agreeing to go?
Is cancer such a sycophant
It had to call dementia
Before moving out of camp?

Spear-bearers for hunters
Like herpes, night-chills and fever
Joined the fray with secret ambitions:
To out-spear the spear wielders
And out-kill the vocational killers.

V

Flies, gnats and mosquitoes
Dreaded pests in their own right
All consider death to be a pest.

The tree groans and cracks
Before it falls.

Fishes of the sea
Fight the rising net
With their bare faces.

The headless chicken
Sprints away from death
After it is already dead.

Perhaps God created us all death-fearing creatures
Then sentenced us to die.

African Tears are Everywhere

The Trans-Atlantic Thief

By what primogeniture
Did you come to inherit
All the beautiful furniture
Of Africa
Especially the land?

Are we consanguineous
Now that you act
On my behalf?

From which gym do you come
Snobbish
And yobbish
That you are?

From where came this snobbery
And forgery
And bribery?

How dare you smash the shrines
And twist the times
Of a people?
How dare you strike at the pates
Of priests?

Did God give you the chain
To yoke other people
And the lock

To keep them chained?

Are we donkeys
That you tantalise
With the very carrots
That we helped to plant?
Are we toddlers
Now that you threaten us
With sugarless tea?

Lords of the universe
Successors of the Romans
Successors of Alexander the Great.
What epitaph shall we write
On your own tombstone
When your time finally comes?

War and Peace

Two engines started
At the very same moment.

One was an engine of war
Gold-geared and gurling the gore
Of the countless murdered.

The other was an engine of peace
Eager like a beaver-on-leash
That throbbed with saintly tune
And was powered by the sweat
And oiled by the toil
of martyrs.

Through bog and panga-cut path
Both engines drove
Mosquito-bitten and tsetse-fly-stung
Both engines strove
Teaching, healing
Stealing, beating.

Brimful-of-sin horse
Neck to neck
with reeling-with-zeal donkey
Cannon conned surplice
Bible blackmailed bayonet.
Spiritual fire-drops flashed
To booms of thundering maxims.

Clash of spear and steel spur
Clamouring like church bell
Kagubi's tears of frustration flowing
With Moleli's tears of repentance
From evil to good and good to evil
Events oscillated
Bringing to each ambience
Essence from the other side.

Two engines started at the very same moment
One was an engine of peace
Powered by prayer and earnest toil
The other was an engine of war
Geared for gold and blazing primrose trails
That soon swallowed the tiny paths of peace
Carved by the saintly engine on leash.

Dangerous Disease

This peeping about
And looking around
For new openings
To enter

Is a dangerous disease
Called economic lechery
Caused by a retrovirus
First discovered
By African scientists
In wild Western monkeys

Dangerous Inertia

This dilly-dallying
And shilly-shallying
About the economic woes
Of Africa

Is like the mumblings
Of a man in his sleep.
It is like the rumblings
Of a confused stomach

And will only end
when the sleeper wakes up
to find his birthright stolen,
or when the stomach finally settles
for a purgative diarrhoea.

Rwanda 1994

Caught between two sharp shards
From the same broken vessel
And cut from either side
Mother weeps because her back is scalded
And baby bawls because his belly is burnt.

The innocent bush is struck
Because there is a hare hiding amongst its leaves.
The thirsty cow is accused of stealing water
Because there is mud on its hooves.
The man who stopped to warm himself by a thief's fire
Is arrested together with the thief
And *tsvukukuviri* the earthworm is killed
Because he resembles a snake.

When civets are skinned in public
And thatches removed to reveal
Embarrassing secrets
Then ask the soil to explain
For it is the soil
And only the soil that knows
When the baby of the mouse is ill.

African Tears are Everywhere

The waters of all seas in the world
Were made from the salty tears
Humans have wept over the centuries.

Indonesian tears
Mauritian tears
African tears
Mixing in the mighty Indian Ocean

Italian tears
Greek tears
Spanish tears
African tears
Comingling in the calm Mediterranean

English tears
American tears
Brazilian tears
Panamanian tears
African tears
Churning within the roiling Atlantic.

The salty waters of almost all seas in the world
Have African tears in them.

Dreams about Women

Questions

Does it not strike you as strange
That we cuddle, kiss and caress
Suck each other's lips in and out
But never look into each other's eyes?

Is it not odd
That we dig into each other's backgrounds
Ask minute details about the past
But never discuss the future
In half as much detail?

Do questions not knock on the door of your mind
When, after spending whole nights
Whispering, cuddling and laughing
We plod wearily across the following days
Like unfamiliar horses
Harnessed to a cumbersome load?

Redmak, Princess of Mutoko

I

This poem is a sigh
Rising from the sepia seams of the heart.
This poem is also a cry
Torn from the deepest tunnels of my soul:
      Mine shaft gas sometimes ignites
      Even when the gentle Davey lamp is used
      As light.

II

No hard words were ever spoken
No cruel looks were even exchanged
But bewitched blood boiling and bursting
The very heart that moved it.

III

Princess of Mutoko
Standing tall like a gazelle
Staring at me with black glowing eyes
That match that patch of sky
Lit by the Milky Way.

Did you notice I loved you with a love so delicate
It fainted on its way out, within my throat?
Did the blood in your veins not warn
That close was a powerful current
Sparking and dangerous
That could send it racing

Like a pack of antelope
Shocked by thunder?

Sweet satsuma
You knew but dared not believe
That you knew.

IV

Shall I out-sigh the sigher of the river
Who lives amongst the reeds,
Or shall I out-cry the crier of a town
Announcing the collapse of the kingdom?

Foolish woman!
Gormless woman!

Do you realise that the very marrow of bones melts
And pours out of my skin
Coating my tongue with flakes of truth?

Are you frozen to the core?
Is this chilly breeze that engulfs me
Fanning out of your nostrils?
Shall my own love be the tattered coat
That I shall wrap around my shoulders?

V

When I think of this still-born love
Which matured for months
But never got to live,

I can only sigh
Like the river sigher
And cry
Like the official crier
Of an apocalyptic town.

When I Woke Up

When I woke up
And knew she was gone
My heart
Was cut out
Weighed
Wrapped up
And transported

Then tossed
Into a seething cauldron
Where it boiled
With herbs and spices

Before being served
To a sybaritic pet
That ate it slowly.

Heartbreak

My heart disintegrates
It breaks into clods
Like a thick podzol
Pierced by the winter plough.

In fragments
Exposed
Turned up-side-down
And inside-out
It can only wait
For the summer rain
To make it whole again.

Dreams about Women

I dreamt woman was a fruity floral plant
Papaya sweet and set to supplant
The marigolds on my windowsill.

I woke up
To find my wife bursting out of her flowerpot
And reaching for native earth
With eager roots.

Dour
And sour
She wielded power
Like a long-hidden brew
Fermented
At the top of a tower.

As she bubbled with effervescence
I took one searing sip of her
And sighed away
My shibboleths.

*In this poem on the rise of feminism, the poet reflects on abandoned
patriarchal views such as the perception that women are contained like
potted plants decorating a windowsill. The illusion is broken when the
poet wakes up to realise that women have broken out of their "flowerpots"
and are forcefully expressing their elemental feminine strength.

So, Let it Be

Conception

Where were you
When that petrified little cell
Stole out of her mother's hut
And pitter-pattered with gingery feet
Down the fallopian way?

Did you share her anxiety
As she approached the uterine gates
To be squashed and flushed
If no opposite cell came to meet her?

Did you participate in the rush
Of the father cells
As they swam for dear life
Knowing they too would perish
If they lost the race?

Were you there to celebrate
When that cell carrying half of you
Met the other half
And there was conception?

Religion

Religion is like an octopus
That wraps multitudinous arms around the neophyte
And will not let go.

Trapped and suffocated
The new believer struggles
For freer space.

But on the day deep-sea sharks attack
The believer snuggles
Within the protective arms
Surrounding them.

The Nemesis

Five lightnings crackled around her head
And charged the air with tension.

Her green eyes
Glowing like phosphorus
Sent purple points of light
Piercing out of the pupils.

Her nostrils when she breathed
Contracted and dilated
Dilated and contracted
Revealing orange insides
That smouldered like fire.

Her red lips, when she spoke
Sent flames more dangerous than those from a flame-thrower
Curling towards the ceiling.

Who was she?
Who else could she be?
But the Nemesis comes to face the man
Who had sweet-talked all of his neighbours' wives
And sired in the surroundings
A whole creche of children.

The Cat

In steel chambers and concrete hutches
Nuclear power purrs like a lazy cat
Fed lavishly on its uranium cheeses.

It grows fatter
And stronger
And readier

To lash out
And blast to dust
The rats that have created it.

Scatterings

When the mace fell upon the block
Chips flew in all directions
Then gathered in a scree
Around their granite God.

Who then is this
Who holds multi-coloured pebbles in his gnarled palm
That he calls his own?

So, Let it Be

As cold winds like to stay
In dark damp caves
And dew, fresh and crystalline
Prefers to hide
Beneath pieces of old decaying bark

Certain beetles
Wise in their own conceit
Love to roll and push
Of all things
Balls of dung!

And certain men
Macho in their self-deceit
Fight pitched battles with knowledge
And commit infanticide
When tiny babes of wisdom
Crawl towards them.

Organising Lines of Poetry

Youthful Vignettes

Youthful vignettes
Falling from poet's pen like petals plucked from pistil by
passing winds
Dry up soon.

The hard pip remains
A stubborn bullet-shaped finger
that points warningly at the sky
and will not fall off
until ripe and mature.

Poetry With a Mission

Crayon poetry
Written in wax
Melts quite fast.

Fibre-tip poetry
Penned in ether
Passes like a fever.

Molten poetry
Mined from the heart
And purified in sweat
Clings to the brow
And colours the vision:
Poetry with a mission.

From the Ashes of my Burnt Hopes

My hopes, burnt to ash by fire
Emulsify with ire
And melt on a pyre
In lines of wavering verse
Which collect in a mire
The sire
Of green writing.

Organising Lines of Poetry

The effort to marshal and organise lines of poetry
Is like trying to control
A class of riotous urchins.

Thoughts and images
Rushing out like savages
Tangle in the passages.

A big idea breaks free
But is held by the snout
And told not to shout
Until a little idea
Still caught in the crowd
Is pulled to the front.

By the time that little idea is extricated
Kicking and swearing
The first big idea has given up
And is sitting on the ground, staring sheepishly
At his aching feet.

Milton Keynes UK
Ingram Content Group UK Ltd.
UKHW011830041023
429950UK00004B/324